History of America

BATTLE AT THE ALAMO

Written by **Teri and Bob Temple**

Educational Media

rourkeeducationalmedia.com

www.rourkeeducationalmedia.com

PHOTO CREDITS: Library of Congress, cover (top left and right and bottom right), 1, 7, 14, 19, 45 (second and third from top), 46 (column one top, second from top, fourth from top, second column, first and second from top), (fourth and fifth from top); Stock Montage, 4-5, 8-9, 20, 26 (bottom left), 44 (bottom);Courtesy of The Center for American History, The University of Texas at Austin, 13, 15, 16, 17, 24, 27 (top), 33, 36-37, 41, 42, 43 (top), 46 (second column third from top); iStockphoto, 10, 21, 27 (bottom), 28, 29, 30, 31, 43; Texas State Library & Archives Commission,12, 26 (top), 39, 44 (top), 45 (top and bottom), 46 (first column second from top); Jim Bowie, Courtesy of the State Preservation Board, Austin, Texas. CHA 2001.4, Photographer Eric Beggs, 6/25/04, post conservation, 25; Dawn at the Alamo, Courtesy of the State Preservation Board, Austin, Texas. CHA 1989.81, Photographer Perry Huston, 8/2/94, post conservation, 32; The Battle of San Jacinto, Courtesy of the State Preservation Board, Austin, Texas. CHA 1989.80, Photographer Perry Huston, 8/3/94, post conservation, 38, 46 (column one bottom)

Edited by Jill Sherman

Cover design by Nicola Stratford, bdpublishing.com

Interior layout by Jen Thomas

Library of Congress PCN Data

Temple, Teri and Bob
  Battle At The Alamo / Teri and Bob Temple
  ISBN 978-1-62169-829-6 (hard cover)
  ISBN 978-1-62169-724-4 (soft cover)
  ISBN 978-1-62169-933-0 (e-Book)
  Library of Congress Control Number: 2013936370

Also Available as:

Rourke Educational Media
Printed in the United States of America,
North Mankato, Minnesota

rourkeeducationalmedia.com
customerservice@rourkeeducationalmedia.com • PO Box 643328 Vero Beach, Florida 32964

TABLE OF CONTENTS

Chapter 1

SNEAK ATTACK

The time had come. In the early morning darkness of March 6, 1836, General Santa Anna made his final move. Under thick cover from passing clouds, the Mexican army crossed the San Antonio River to close in on the Alamo fort. The soldiers silently waited for the signal to attack, their **bayonets** ready.

Inside the walls of the Alamo all was quiet. The Mexicans had been firing nonstop at the fort for 12 days. The men inside were so exhausted they had fallen asleep at their posts. Even the three lookouts stationed outside the fort's walls failed to detect the enemy's movements.

General Santa Anna (1794–1876)

General Santa Anna had pulled it off. His army sat within one **musket** shot's distance of the Alamo. The element of surprise was on their side.

The first bits of light streaked the sky when Santa Anna gave the signal to attack. A bugle's call to arms rang through the air. The 1,400 Mexican soldiers moved toward the fort.

Captain John Baugh was keeping watch along the walls of the Alamo when he heard the bugle's call. He gazed out into the darkness surrounding the fort. Hearing the approaching enemy, he shouted, "The Mexicans are coming!"

"After a long wait we took our places at three o'clock a.m. on the south side, a distance of 300 feet from the fort of the enemy. Here we remained flat on our stomachs until 5:30 (Whew! it was cold) when the signal to march was given by the President from the battery."

Mexican soldier in a letter to fellow soldiers at San Antonio de Béxar.

The Battle of the Alamo was a costly win for Santa Anna. He lost about 600 soldiers to some 200 rebellious Texans.

The people inside were jolted from their sleep by the sound of soldiers yelling, *"Viva Santa Anna! Viva Mexico!"* Long live Santa Anna! Long live Mexico! Fear surged through the Texans as they heard the Mexican military band playing the Deguello. This music was an **ancient** call to fight to the death, showing no mercy. Santa Anna hoped it would give his men courage as they charged the walls.

THE MEN OF THE ALAMO

The men inside the Alamo all had different reasons for responding to the call to aid Texas in its fight for independence from Mexico. Most of them hoped victory would allow them to own land. Some were defending land they already owned. Others fought for their rights, and still others sought glory or a chance to escape their past. Like the people of the United States, the defenders of the Alamo were a diverse group. The Alamo volunteers and soldiers came from at least 22 states and as many as six foreign countries. The only native-born Texans among them were the nine Tejanos, Mexicans who had settled in the area. This group ranged in age from 16 to 57; the average age was only 29. Most of the men were frontiersmen, fur trappers, and hunters from the southwestern United States. A few were doctors or lawyers.

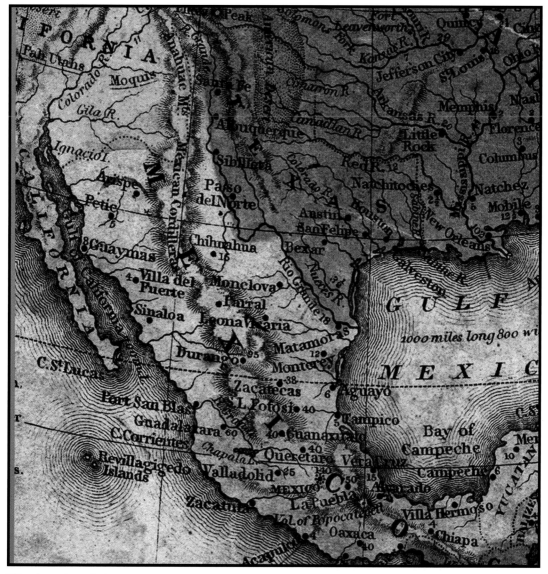

The Battle of the Alamo was a pivotal event in the Texas Revolution.

The battle that followed held the fate of Texas in its bloody grip. Would Texas gain its independence? Would Mexico continue to rule the land? The defenders of the Alamo would not survive the battle. Their defeat, however, set the stage for a victory that would change the course of U.S. history.

Chapter 2

THE ROAD LEADING TO WAR

In the early sixteenth century, a group of Spanish explorers passed through parts of the area and claimed the land for Spain even though Native Americans had lived on the land for thousands of years. By the late seventeenth century, Spain had begun setting up missions in the region.

The missions were meant to convert the Native Americans to Catholicism and make them loyal to Spanish rule. The missions weren't just churches. They were large, walled-in compounds where an entire religious community lived and worked.

In 1718, Spain built one such mission along the San Antonio River. It was called San Antonio de Valero. In the beginning, the mission was nothing more than a straw building, but it would eventually become the Alamo. Its high walls would make it useful as a fort for staging battle. A town sprang up across the river and took the name San Antonio de Béxar. Today it is known simply as San Antonio.

More than 2.5 million people a year visit the 4.2 acre (1.7 hectare) complex in downtown San Antonio, Texas known worldwide as the Alamo.

"Our rifles are by our side, and choice guns they are, we know what awaits us, and are prepared to meet it."

Letter from Daniel William Cloud of Kentucky, a defender of the Alamo, dated December 26, 1835, on the way to San Antonio.

The Caddo people were one of the groups native to Texas and are credited with giving the area its name. Tejas is the Spanish spelling of a Caddo word that means friend. Early Spanish explorers began calling the whole region Tejas after the people they had met there. Over time the pronunciation changed to Texas.

The city and the mission were ruled by Spain for more than a hundred years. When Mexico won its independence from Spain in 1821, it gained control of the land that is now Texas, including San Antonio and the Alamo.

In 1833, General Antonio López de Santa Anna rose to power in Mexico. Santa Anna encouraged his people to settle the lands to the northwest, the area that is now Texas. The Mexicans who lived in the region came to be called Tejanos. They were mainly cattle ranchers who lived peacefully with the few Americans who had traveled west to settle there. The new Mexican government also encouraged Americans to settle in Texas by offering them free land. By 1835, there were almost ten times as many English-speaking Texans as Spanish-speaking Tejanos.

In the beginning, the Mexican government didn't enforce many rules in the new American settlements. Over time, however, Mexican leaders began to feel they were losing control of Texas. Settlers were buying up too much land. Many refused to pay taxes.

> The Mission San Antonio de Valero came to be called the Alamo by a group of Spanish soldiers stationed nearby. They named it in honor of their hometown, Alamo de Parras. Alamo is the Spanish word for cottonwood. The Alamo eventually became the mission's official name.

In 1830, the Mexican government stopped allowing U.S. citizens to settle in Texas. Existing laws were now strictly observed, and Mexico demanded payment of taxes. To enforce the new rules, Santa Anna sent small numbers of troops to the region.

The stiffer rules made the settlers unhappy and gave rise to two political parties. The people of the War Party felt that Texas should be independent from Mexico, even if it meant going to war. The Peace Party urged citizens to remain loyal to Mexico and felt that a peaceful solution could be reached.

Mexican commander Santa Anna and his general surrendered to American leader Samuel Houston after the Battle of San Jacinto in April 1836.

Stephen Austin (1793–1836)

Stephen Austin, who had worked with the Mexican government to encourage Americans to come to the area, belonged to the Peace Party. He traveled to Mexico to plead the case of the settlers. Santa Anna did not see Austin as a peacemaker and had him jailed for stirring up revolution. Austin soon changed his opinion about independence. When he returned to Texas, he encouraged his fellow Texans to go to war with Mexico.

"I must say as to what I have seen of Texas it is the garden spot of the world. The best land and best prospects for health I ever saw and I do so believe it is a fortune to any man to come here. There is a world of country to Settle."

Letter from Davy Crockett to his son and daughter, San Augustine, Texas, January 9, 1836.

"The cause of Philanthropy, of Humanity, of Liberty & human happiness throughout the world call loudly on every man to come to aid Texas."

Letter written by Daniel William Cloud, December 26, 1835.

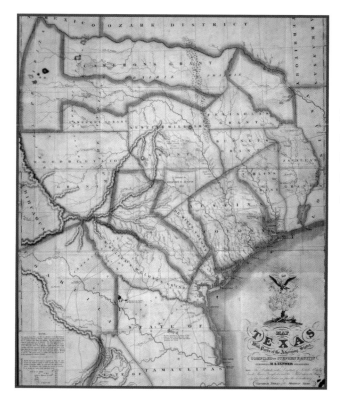

Stephen Austin, known as the Father of Texas, created this map of Texas in 1822 when the region was still under Mexican control.

Meanwhile, Santa Anna sent General Martín Perfecto de Cos, along with hundreds of troops, to establish a headquarters in the town of San Antonio de Béxar. Tensions increased when Santa Anna sent soldiers to retrieve an old cannon from the Texan settlement of Gonzales. Instead of handing the cannon over peacefully, the angry **colonists** filled it with scrap iron and nails to use against the Mexican troops. They proudly waved a homemade flag bearing the words COME AND TAKE IT! The colonists won the Battle at Gonzales. The shot from that cannon went on to start the Texas Revolution.

Samuel Houston (1793–1863)

In November 1835, a group of 57 Texan leaders met and wrote the Declaration of Causes. The document listed the reasons they were rebelling and called for all of Texas to join together in the fight. They also established a separate government and elected Henry Smith as the first governor. Sam Houston was made the commander-in-chief of the rebel Texan army.

In December 1835, the Texan and Tejano revolutionaries fought the Mexican troops that had settled in San Antonio de Béxar. For five days the battle raged. After forcing General Cos and his troops to surrender and leave, the rebels took control of the Alamo.

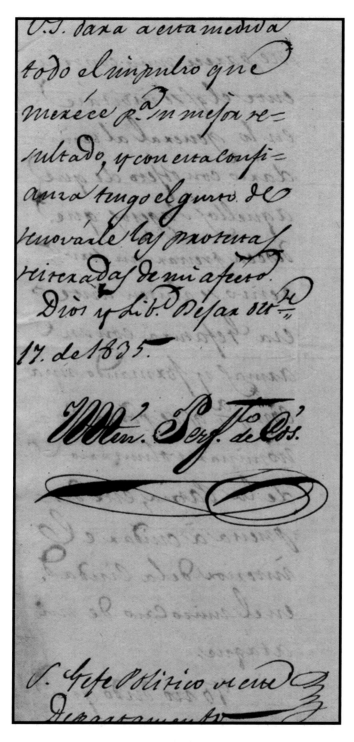

General Martín Perfecto de Cos wrote this letter to a fellow Mexican official at San Antonio de Béxar on October 17, 1835. General Cos called upon the people of the city to rally against the rebel colonists. However, the Texas rebels captured the city soon afterward.

Chapter 3

SANTA ANNA'S MISSION TO RECLAIM TEXAS

Davy Crockett (1786–1836)

Santa Anna had many reasons to attack the Alamo. He saw the rebels as ungrateful villains. He thought they had accepted Mexico's generous offer of land only to betray the nation. They dared to attack his army at Gonzales and had humiliated General Cos at Béxar. Santa Anna knew a victory at the Alamo would deliver a strong message to the rebels. It was also his chance to kill the Texan leaders who were stationed there, including Jim Bowie, Buck Travis, and Davy Crockett.

Many of Santa Anna's officers felt he should ignore the Alamo. It was not a significant fort, and they worried the battle would cost too many Mexican lives. They wanted to attack more important cities to the east.

But Santa Anna planned to take back the town of San Antonio de Béxar and make an example of those at the Alamo. As the head of the Mexican government, he intended to show no mercy. The rebel Texans and Tejanos would have to surrender completely or die fighting.

Because Santa Anna's goal was to take the rebels by surprise, he decided to attack in winter, when they would not be expecting it. In late January he began marching several thousand of his men toward San Antonio de Béxar. He knew the unpredictable weather would make for a difficult trip, but his desire for speed left him unprepared for the journey. The group of mostly untrained men were short on supplies, and only one doctor traveled with them. They lost hundreds of men, and many more left the army rather than march to their deaths.

> "The foreigners who are making war on the Mexican nation in violation of every rule of law are entitled to no consideration whatever, and in consequence no quarter is to be given them."
>
> *General Santa Anna's orders to his army.*

General Martín Perfecto de Cos (1800–1854)

The Mexican army was very particular about the size of its soldiers. They carefully measured each man's height. The desire was to keep the average height between 5 feet and 5 feet, 6 inches tall (between 152 and 165 centimeters). That way Santa Anna was sure to be one of the tallest men in the army. He stood 5 feet, 10 inches (178 centimeters) tall.

On February 23, 1836, Santa Anna and his army finally arrived in San Antonio de Béxar. There, he raised a red banner high above the San Fernando Church. Situated only 800 yards (732 meters) from the Alamo, the rebels could not miss his message: surrender or die.

Originally known as Mission San Antonio de Valero, the former Roman Catholic mission and fortress compound lay in ruins after the Battle of the Alamo.

Chapter 4
PREPARING FOR BATTLE

The Texans also prepared for war. Some of the rebels wanted to take the fight all the way to Mexico. This caused a great deal of conflict in the rebel government, as people argued over what their next step should be. The Texan army was in chaos. Some of the force stationed at the Alamo began to strip it of supplies, preparing to carry them toward a battle in Mexico. Colonel James C. Neill was left in charge of San Antonio de Béxar and the Alamo, along with fewer than a hundred men. In desperate need of soldiers and supplies, he wrote to Sam Houston looking for assistance.

Cannons used in the Battle of the Alamo can be seen today on Alamo Plaza in downtown San Antonio, Texas.

Houston knew that the victory at the Battle of Gonzales was temporary. Mexican forces were sure to return, and he had to decide which forts to defend and which ones to leave. He sent Jim Bowie on an expedition to determine the fate of the Alamo. Bowie arrived at the fort with 30 or so men. He told Houston he wanted to stay and defend the Alamo rather than tear it down.

VOLUNTEERS BOUND BY AN OATH

Because the majority of the men inside the Alamo were volunteers, people sometimes think they could have left at any time. In nineteenth-century military terms a volunteer was a citizen-soldier. These men each signed an oath of allegiance to the rebel government of Texas stating, "I will serve her honestly and faithfully against all her enemies and opposers whatsoever, and observe and obey the orders of the Governor of Texas, the orders and decrees of the present and future authorities and the orders of the officers appointed over me according to the rules and regulations for the government of Texas."

The volunteers took their oath seriously. They stayed on in the fort through hardship and battle. But others, who had not taken an oath, could come and go out freely. Some of these people were pro-Mexican, and they informed Santa Anna about the rebels and their activities inside the fort.

Following Bowie's recommendation, Governor Smith sent Lieutenant Colonel William "Buck" Travis along with 30 more men to the Alamo to help Neill. Travis's party arrived on February 3, 1836. Davy Crockett arrived at the fort on February 8 along with 12 Tennessee mountain men, who were known for their shooting skills. Once there he declared, "I have come to aid you all that I can in your noble cause."

In the following days, a struggle for leadership arose within the Alamo. A family crisis caused Neill to step down from his post, leaving Travis in command. The volunteers preferred Bowie as their leader, however, so the two men had to work out a solution. Travis was put in charge of the regular army, while Bowie led the volunteer fighters. This decided, they set about preparing the Alamo for battle.

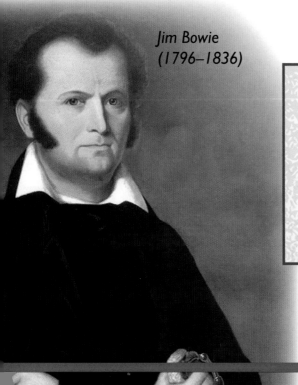

Jim Bowie
(1796–1836)

"As I ran across the Main Plaza, I saw a splendid sight. A large army was coming toward me on horseback and on foot. They wore red coats and blue trousers with white bands across their chests. Pennants were flying and swords sparkled in the bright winter sky."

Enrique Esparza, a pro-Mexican resident of Texas, in a 1907 account of the siege, published in the San Antonio Express.

Lieutenant Colonel William "Buck" Travis
(1809–1836)

Susanna Dickinson (1814–1883)

"Captain Dickinson galloped up to our dwelling and hurriedly exclaimed:
'The Mexicans are upon us, give me the babe, and jump up behind me.'
I did so, and as the Mexicans already occupied Commerce street, we
galloped across the river at the ford south of it, and entered the fort
at the southern gate, when the enemy commenced firing shot and shell
into the fort, but with little or no effect, only wounding one horse."

Mrs. Susanna Dickinson, 1875.

Chapter 5
SANTA ANNA SURROUNDS THE ALAMO

Santa Anna stationed his troops around the fort as he waited for the rest of his men to arrive. Now it would be difficult for Alamo defenders to come and go, and supplies could not easily be brought in. Santa Anna's plan was to wear down and starve the rebels, forcing them to surrender. If that didn't work he would attack.

Soon Jim Bowie collapsed. He had been fighting an illness for weeks, possibly tuberculosis. Now his strength was leaving him. Bowie was moved to a cot in a separate building, which he would never leave again.

> "The enemy has demanded a surrender...I have answered the demand with a cannon shot, & our flag still waves proudly from the walls—I shall never surrender or retreat."
>
> *Letter from William Travis to the*
> *"People of Texas and All Americans in the World," February 24, 1836.*

Jim Bowie's trademark knife, called a "Bowie knife" in his honor.

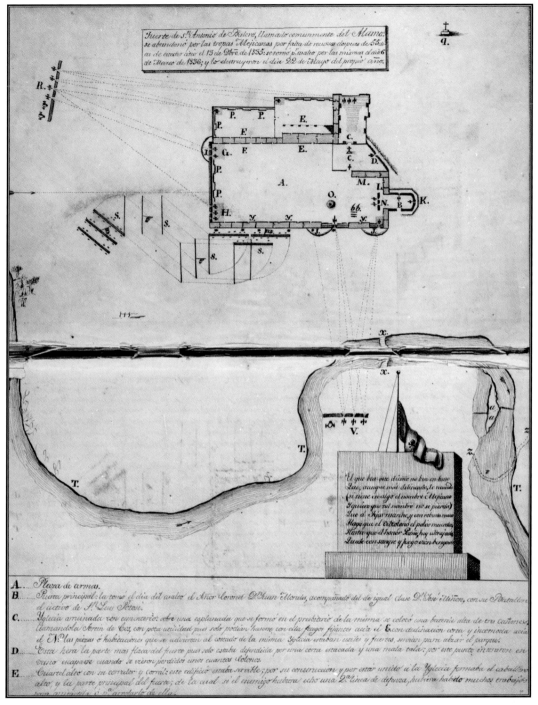

Sánchez Navarro kept a private record and plan of the Alamo, identifying the fort's physical components and its defenses, with comments on their relative strengths.

Bowie's last official act as co-commander of the fort was to give William Travis full leadership. Travis rose to the occasion. He set the men to strengthening the walls of the fort, especially the crumbling north wall. The work was done amid almost constant cannon fire by the Mexican army. Because of the limited amount of gunpowder in the fort, Travis ordered his troops to hold their fire until the real attack came. Each day Travis ordered three cannon shots. This let the people in the countryside know that the rebels were still hanging on.

KEEPING SPIRITS UP

Davy Crockett helped with the frustration and boredom of the men inside the fort by entertaining them with his elaborate tales of adventure. He also played the fiddle and would engage in musical duels with Scottish born John McGregor on bagpipes to see who was louder.

Davy Crockett
1786–1836

But the games could not hide the truth. Mexican troops were entering Béxar by the hundreds each day. Confined to a small area, tired and hungry, the spirits of the men of the Alamo sank as they pondered two questions: When would Santa Anna attack? Would any help arrive in time?

TEXAS
FOREVER!!

The usurper of the South has failed in his efforts to enslave the freemen of Texas.

The wives and daughters of Texas will be saved from the brutality of Mexican soldiers.

Now is the time to emigrate to the Garden of America.

A free passage, and all found, is offered at New Orleans to all applicants. Every settler receives a location of

EIGHT HUNDRED ACRES OF LAND.

On the 23d of February, a force of 1000 Mexicans came in sight of San Antonio, and on the 25th Gen. St. Anna arrived at that place with 2500 more men, and demanded a surrender of the fort held by 150 Texians, and on the refusal, he attempted to storm the fort, twice, with his whole force, but was repelled with the loss of 500 men, and the Americans lost none. Many of his troops, the liberals of Zacatecas, are brought on to Texas in irons and are urged forward with the promise of the women and plunder of Texas.

The Texian forces were marching to relieve St. Antonio, March the 2d. The Government of Texas is supplied with plenty of arms, ammunition, provisions, &c. &c.

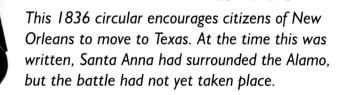

This 1836 circular encourages citizens of New Orleans to move to Texas. At the time this was written, Santa Anna had surrounded the Alamo, but the battle had not yet taken place.

On the eighth day, the rebels received a boost when 32 men arrived from Gonzales on the morning of March 1, 1836. Still, there were fewer than 200 troops inside the Alamo. The men hoped for more reinforcements, but they would be disappointed.

The conditions inside the fort grew worse. The water supply had run dry and they lacked firewood. Despite the fact that the Mexican army had them surrounded, some of the rebels were able to sneak out of the compound to obtain these necessary supplies. Travis also smuggled out letters begging for aid.

More than 2.5 million visitors come from all over the world to stand before the old stones of the Alamo and honor the courage and sacrifice of the defenders.

Today the Alamo buildings surround a green courtyard.

As the situation worsened, Travis sent one final letter to David Ayres, a friend who was caring for Travis's young son. Written on March 3, it said, "Take care of my little boy. If the country should be saved, I may make him a splendid fortune; but if the country should be lost and I should perish, he will have nothing but the proud recollection that he is the son of a man who died for his country."

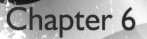

Chapter 6

FINAL BATTLE AT THE ALAMO

In the predawn hours of March 6, 1836, the Alamo defenders waited inside the mission. They had been under **siege** for an agonizing 13 days. By 5 a.m., almost 2,400 Mexican soldiers surrounded the fort. The exhausted men inside did not know so many Mexican soldiers had arrived. Many of the defenders were sick, and they were extremely unprepared. Santa Anna had planned well. Most of his men waited in four well-placed columns for the call to attack.

While the Alamo defenders waited for an attack, they readied their supplies, stacking cannonballs, cleaning rifles, and strengthening the fort walls.

This 1912 painting shows the hand-to-hand combat during the last moments of the battle at the Alamo.

At 5:30 a.m., Santa Anna gave the buglers the order. Sounds of the Deguello rang out. Santa Anna's troops charged the Alamo. The sound of the battle song echoed around them as each unit's bugler picked up the call and played it, over and over. The final battle had begun.

The music alerted the Texans, who pointed their rifles and cannons toward the sound. The first column of Mexican soldiers was wiped out before they reached the fort's walls. As Santa Anna sent wave after wave of soldiers toward the fort, sharp-shooting frontiersmen along the tops of the walls picked them off.

The Battle at the Alamo became a popular subject for artists. This painting from around 1905 shows the ferocity of the battle that left a substantial legacy and influence within American culture.

Cannon fire lit the early-morning sky. Travis quickly realized the difficulty he faced. He could see Santa Anna's men surrounding the fort. He knew that as soon as they reached the walls, the rebels' long rifles would be useless. Only by leaning over the edge and exposing himself to deadly musket fire could Travis hope to help his men. He did just that, firing point-blank at the Mexican soldiers who were attempting to scale the wall with ladders. Finally, he was struck in the head by a single shot of enemy fire. He tumbled back and fell across his cannon, becoming one of the first Texan casualties of the battle.

José Enrique de la Peña, one of Santa Anna's officers, wrote an account of the Battle of the Alamo. The pages shown here describe the death of William Travis.

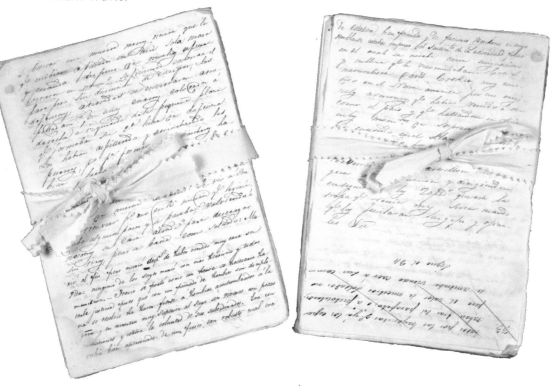

The Fall of the Alamo *by Robert Jenkins Onderdonk depicts Davy Crockett swinging his rifle at Mexican troops who breached the south gate of the mission.*

The Mexican army faced many casualties as well. Shaken and frustrated, Santa Anna sent his army back to the town to regroup. There he raised their spirits and helped them regain their confidence. With renewed courage they once again stormed the fort. Still, the Mexican troops were being killed at an alarming rate. At least one-fourth of all the casualties suffered by Santa Anna's army were caused by friendly fire, misguided shots from their own guns.

The turning point came just when it seemed the Mexicans would have to give up. Santa Anna sent in a group of men to help knock down a section of the north wall, which was the weakest point in the fort. The men swarmed in, forcing the rebels to **retreat** farther inside. Meanwhile, a group of men led by General Cos found a way to break the west wall. Using axes and crowbars, they smashed **barricades** that covered the windows. They climbed through the gunports and scrambled over the wall into the compound.

The defenders, realizing the enemy was now inside the fort, barricaded themselves inside the mission's buildings. They gathered in the long barracks and church to fight. Here they would make their last stand.

The Texans had managed to hold their ground for a short while. However, they were no match for the advancing soldiers. The Mexicans used the rebels' own cannons to blast through the doors of the buildings. As the cannonballs pounded away, Santa Anna's army rushed into the rooms, stabbing any men they found with their bayonets.

In the fort, the fight was furious. No longer able to fire their long rifles, the rebels used knives and **tomahawks** in hand-to-hand combat but were quickly defeated. Although the battle lasted only minutes, the carnage left behind was horrible to behold. Alamo defenders and Mexicans alike lay dead all over the fort and its surrounding fields.

THE STORY OF JUAN SEGUÍN

Juan Seguín, a Tejano, was one of the most loyal rebels of the Texas Revolution. He strongly supported the cause of Texas independence and joined the Texas army as a captain.

During the siege by the Mexican army, Alamo leaders sent Seguín out to retrieve supplies. Seguín wanted to stay and help defend the fort, but he was the best choice because of his familiarity with the surrounding land. Little did he know, the leaders' decision would save his life.

Juan Seguín (1806–1890)

Seguín was not at the fort when the Mexican army attacked. He made his way to San Jacinto, where he met up with Sam Houston. Hoping to avenge all the friends he had lost at the Alamo, Seguín joined Houston's army. Seguín was among the fighters who would eventually defeat Santa Anna's army.

After Texas won its independence, relations between the American-born Texans and the Mexican-born Tejanos became strained. As a Tejano, Seguín experienced discrimination in Texas and eventually fled to Mexico.

A wood engraving from 1837 showing the execution of Davy Crockett by Mexican soldiers.

> "Some seven men had survived the general carnage and …they were brought before Santa Anna. …Though tortured before they were killed, these unfortunates died without complaining and without humiliating themselves before their torturers."
>
> *José Enrique de la Peña, one of Santa Anna's staff officers, describing in his diary the last moments of a group of Texan prisoners-of-war.*

No one will ever know for sure how many died at the Alamo that day. It is believed that between 190 and 260 Americans were killed. Santa Anna's losses were far greater. Of the nearly 2,400 Mexican soldiers, as many as 600 were killed and hundreds more were wounded.

A small group of defenders, including Davy Crockett, had been captured that morning and brought before Santa Anna himself. Some of his officers begged him to show mercy on the prisoners, but Santa Anna ordered all the rebels executed. He then had the mayor of the town walk him around the fort, pointing out the fallen bodies of the revolutionary leaders.

Chapter 7
TEXANS TAKE REVENGE

Following the battle, Santa Anna sent for the survivors of the Alamo, including Susanna Dickinson, the only white woman to survive the attack. She unwillingly became a messenger for Santa Anna, who wanted to spread news of the Mexican victory. He sent Dickinson to the town of Gonzales to tell the story to General Sam Houston and any other Texan who would listen. Santa Anna hoped it would serve as a warning about what they could expect if they continued to rebel.

Santa Anna marched his army to Goliad. There they overtook the fort and captured more than 400 Texan soldiers. To send another message to the Texans, Santa Anna ordered nearly all of the prisoners executed. The citizens of Texas were outraged and would not stand for this barbaric treatment.

Santa Anna was sure he had stamped out the rebellion through his victories at the Alamo and Goliad, but he wasn't finished. He wanted to defeat Sam Houston's army. Santa Anna sent his soldiers east with orders to destroy every town in their path.

Texans across the region fled their homes in fear, sure that Santa Anna was right behind them. This hasty escape, known as the Runaway Scrape, cost many colonists their lives. Panicked and traveling in heavy rains, they tried to cross dangerously swollen rivers. Many drowned while others

caught terrible diseases. Santa Anna followed closely on their heels, crushing everything in his path.

Sam Houston assembled the male settlers into an army that could challenge Santa Anna. More than 200 of the men came from Gonzales. They had intended to help defend the Alamo but didn't get there in time.

Houston's army was forced to retreat as they waited for the right moment to fight. The group was full of new recruits, so Houston used the time to train them. Neither the government of the new **republic** nor the rebels themselves understood what Houston's plan was. Many called him a coward for retreating.

Houston's army finally took a stand on April 19, 1836. After seeing that the Mexican army was divided into three parts, the commander grabbed his chance while the enemy was not at full strength. His plan was to attack the Mexican soldiers near the San Jacinto River during their afternoon nap. As Houston lead the attack, his men cried out, "Remember the Alamo!" The rebels easily defeated the startled soldiers and took revenge on their counterparts, killing nearly all of the Mexican soldiers.

Santa Anna however, tried to escape. He disgusted himself as a low-ranking soldier. He might have gotten away, but one of his own men recognizes him and yelled, *"Viva el Presidente!"* Long live the president! He was captured and forced to withdraw all of his troops in exchange for his life. He later signed the Treaty of Velasco, which recognized Texas as an independent state.

For 10 years the Republic of Texas had its own government and created its own monetary system. Finally, on December 29, 1845, Texas was admitted into the United States.

SLAVERY IN TEXAS

"Texas was considered the last frontier of slavery in the United States. For more than 50 years, slavery existed because the people of Texas felt it was a necessary to run their land. The original Austin colony had 443 slaves out of a total population of 1,800.

At the time of the Texas Revolution, slavery had been outlawed by the Mexican government. Many in the U.S. Congress, led by former president John Quincy Adams, felt that the fight for independence was fueled by Texans' desire to keep slaves again.

John Quincy Adams (1767–1848)

Texas probably would have become a state sooner had it not been for the slavery issue. In 1844, when Texas was requesting admittance into the United States, the balance of slave and free states was equal. Allowing Texas into the **Union** would tip the balance in favor of slavery.

Eventually the free states agreed to let Texas join the Union. The slave issue was far from over, though, and would eventually lead to a divided nation and civil war in 1861.

BIOGRAPHIES

Many people played important roles throughout this time period. Learn more about them in the Biographies section.

Crockett, David "Davy" (1786–1836) - Davy Crockett has risen to the status of folk hero in Texas history. He was born in the backwoods of Tennessee. By the age of 13, he had earned a reputation as a sharpshooter and skilled hunter. His popularity and famous adventures helped land him a seat in both the Tennessee state legislature and the U.S . House of Representatives. After losing his bid for a fourth term in Congress, he headed for Texas in search of fortune. There, he joined in the Texas Revolution. He was executed by Santa Anna following the defeat at the Alamo.

Austin, Stephen Fuller (1793–1836) - Austin is a major figure in Texas history. Before devoting his life to bringing settlers to Texas, he served in the Missouri legislature and worked as a banker and a judge. Austin established a colony in Texas, a project his father had started before he died. During the Texas Revolution, Austin spent his time trying to gain U.S. support. He was made secretary of state to the Republic of Texas but died several months later.

Houston, Sam (1793–1863) - In the early 1830s, Houston traveled to Texas and found the land of promise. During the Texas Revolution he served as commander-in-chief of the Texas army. He will always be remembered for his defeat of Santa Anna at the Battle of San Jacinto. Sam Houston was twice elected president of the Republic of Texas.

Santa Anna, General Antonio López de (1794–1876) - Santa Anna led the Mexican army during the Texas Revolution. Santa Anna had fought against Spain during Mexico's fight for independence from 1810 to 1821. In 1833, he was elected president of Mexico. He led the army that stormed the Alamo. Santa Anna was forced to resign as president after his capture and defeat at the Battle of San Jacinto. Over the next 20 years he would regain and then lose power and favor with the people of Mexico.

Bowie, James "Jim" (1796–1836) - Bowie was born in Kentucky but was raised in southeastern Louisiana, where he earned his reputation as a street fighter and fearless adventurer. In 1830, Bowie moved to Texas and made a fortune by buying and selling land. While in Texas, he joined in the fight for Texas's independence from Mexico. He rose to the rank of colonel and was in command of the volunteers at the Alamo. Bowie had been disabled by disease, possibly tuberculosis, and was confined to his cot during the siege. He was found dead in his cot at the end of the battle.

Travis, William "Buck" (1809–1836) - Travis, who was born in South Carolina, is best remembered as the Texas army commander in charge of the Alamo during the siege and battle of 1836. One of the first to join Texans in their fight for independence, he quickly rose through the ranks of their army. He was one of the first Texans killed at the Alamo.

Dickinson, Susanna (1814–1883) - Dickinson and her 15-month-old daughter, Angelina, were in the chapel with the other women and children when the Mexican army stormed the Alamo. She and her daughter were among the few survivors. Santa Anna sent her out to tell the story of the attack as a warning to Texan rebels. Instead, she became known as the "messenger of the Alamo" and her story helped stir a nation to action.

TIMELINE

1691
Spanish explorers arrive at present-day San Antonio.

1718
Construction of the Mission San Antonio de Valero (the Alamo) begins.

1821
Stephen Austin brings the first colonists to Texas.

October 2, 1835
The Texas Revolution begins in a fight between Mexican soldiers and the people of Gonzales.

February 23, 1836
General Santa Anna's army arrives outside San Antonio and begins its siege of the Alamo.

March 2, 1836
The Texas Declaration of Independence is signed at Washington-on-the-Brazos.

March 6, 1836
Mexican forces overwhelm and take the Alamo.

March 27, 1836
Some 350 Texans are executed at Goliad.

April 21, 1836
Santa Anna is captured at the Battle of San Jacinto.

December 29, 1845
The United States admits Texas into the Union as the twenty-eighth state.

REFERENCE

Map of the American Southwest
during the Battle of the Alamo

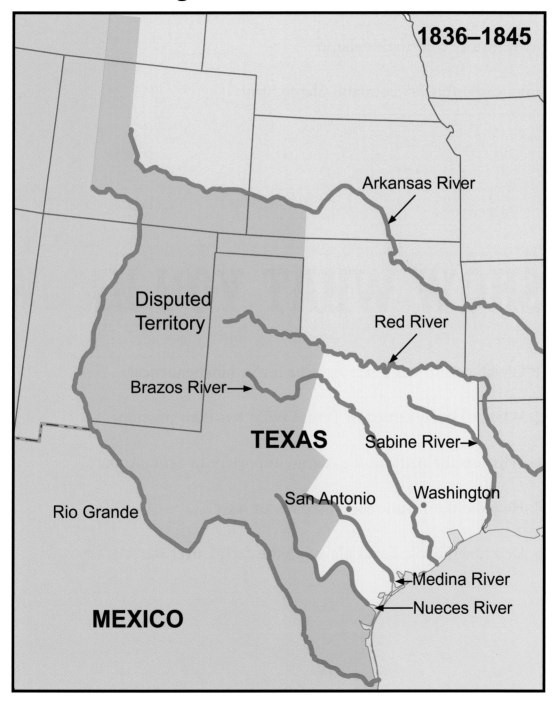

1836–1845

Arkansas River

Disputed
Territory

Red River

Brazos River →

TEXAS

Sabine River →

San Antonio

Washington

Rio Grande

Medina River

Nueces River

MEXICO

WEBSITES TO VISIT

www.thealamo.org

www.history.com/topics/alamo

americasbesthistory.com/abh-alamo.html

SHOW WHAT YOU KNOW

1. Which nation was Texas fighting for its independence?

2. Who originally settled in Texas? What was their mission?

3. Why was the Battle at the Alamo important to Santa Anna?

4. How did the Texan rebels prepare for war?

5. Describe the role Texas played in the debate over slavery.

GLOSSARY

ancient (AYN-shuhnt): very old; something belonging to a long time ago

barricades (BAR-uh-kaydz): barriers to stop people from going past a certain point

bayonets (BAY-uh-nehts): blades attached to the end of a rifle for hand-to-hand combat

colonists (KOL-uh-nihsts): people who settle in a distant land while remaining a citizen of another; before independence, Texans were colonists of Mexico

musket (MUS-kiht): a firearm with a long barrel that was held over the shoulder while firing

republic (ree-PUHB-lik): a form of government that is run by the people and those they elect; the leader of a republic is an elected official rather than a king or queen

retreat (ruh-TREET): to back away from a difficult situation

siege (SEEJ): a military operation in which an important enemy building or area is surrounded and cut off in such a way that supplies cannot easily be brought in; the idea is to slowly wear down the enemy and have them surrender without going to battle

tomahawk (TOM-uh-hawks): small axes originally used by American Indians as a tool or weapon

Union (YOON-yuhn): another name for the United States, especially during the first half of the nineteenth century

INDEX